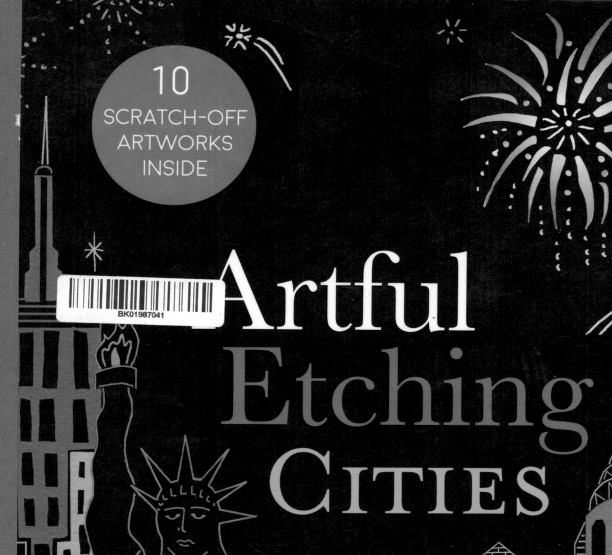

10
SCRATCH-OFF
ARTWORKS
INSIDE

BK01987041

D0204474

Artful
Etching
CITIES

MOHAN
BALLARD

Artful
Etching
CITIES

Thunder Bay Press
An imprint of Printers Row Publishing Group
10350 Barnes Canyon Road, Suite 100, San Diego, CA 92121
www.thunderbaybooks.com

Copyright © 2018 Quarto Publishing plc

All rights reserved. No part of this publication may be reproduced, distributed, or transmitted in any form or by any means, including photocopying, recording, or other electronic or mechanical methods, without the prior written permission of the publisher, except in the case of brief quotations embodied in critical reviews and certain other noncommercial uses permitted by copyright law.

Printers Row Publishing Group is a division of Readerlink Distribution Services, LLC. Thunder Bay Press is a registered trademark of Readerlink Distribution Services, LLC.

All notations of errors or omissions should be addressed to Thunder Bay Press, Editorial Department, at the above address. All other correspondence (author inquiries, permissions) concerning the content of this book should be addressed to: The Bright Press an imprint of The Quarto Group, Ovest House, 58 West Street, Brighton, BN1 2RA, UK.

Thunder Bay Press
Publisher: Peter Norton
Associate Publisher: Ana Parker
Publishing/Editorial Team: April Farr,
Kelly Larsen, Kathryn C. Dalby
Editorial Team: JoAnn Padgett,
Melinda Allman, Dan Mansfield

The Bright Press
Publisher: Mark Searle
Associate Publisher: Emma Bastow
Managing Editor: Isheeta Mustafi
Editor: Caroline Elliker
Design: Eoghan O'Brien
Artwork: Mohan Ballard, Jacqueline Colley

ISBN: 978-1-68412-575-3
Printed in China
22 21 20 19 18 1 2 3 4 5

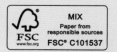
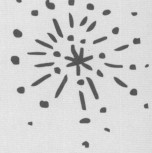

Artful Etching

Scratch the artwork to reveal amazing city skylines!

Welcome to the colorful world of Artful Etching. Use the wooden stylus to create your own amazing works of art, ready to frame and hang on your wall.

How to use this book

This book contains 20 pages of instructions followed by 10 beautiful etching boards. The boards can be easily removed from the book just like the pages of any artist's pad.

Take one of the etching boards from the book and use the wooden stylus to scratch away areas of the black coating, revealing the colored areas underneath. By making different crosshatches, checkerboard patterns, dashes, crosses, brick patterns, circles, dots, and chevrons, you can create stunning city skylines.

The more black you scratch away, the more colorful and dynamic your picture will become—there's no wrong way to do it!

About the artworks

Each of the ten artworks in this book are accompanied by an inspiring tutorial on how to get started, with a detailed description of the marks and artistic lines you can use.

Turn to page 4 to get started in Rio de Janeiro. You can see the **finished artwork** as a guide on the left-hand page, and on the right, you can see a **before and after** that explains how the effects were made. Follow the instructions provided or go your own way to make your own magical cityscapes!

Flip to page 24 to see a gallery of inspiration (this page also highlights where you can find the instructions for each artwork).

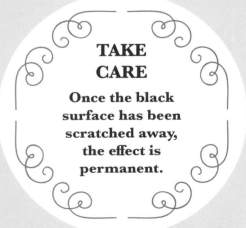

TAKE CARE

Once the black surface has been scratched away, the effect is permanent.

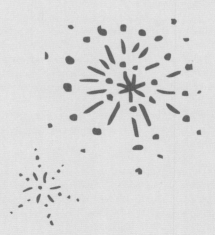

How to Etch

There are so many wonderful ways to use this book. You can scratch away large areas of the black surface to make a bold and colorful design, or simply fill each outline with a different kind of simple mark—crosses, chevrons, dots, brick patterns, circles, and so much more! Here are some handy hints to get you started.

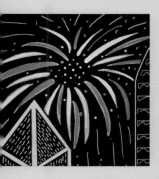

1. Vary the pressure

By applying different amounts of pressure while using the wooden stylus, you can make finer or bolder lines on the page. From strong, straight lines to fine doodles, the etching board is your playground. Use the lightest pressure, then return to the parts of each line where you want to show more color.

2. Make your mark!

The easiest way to get started is by echoing the outlines provided on the boards. Use the wooden stylus to reveal whole buildings or landmarks.

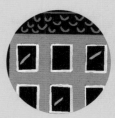

3. Add details

Rather than scratching out whole areas, add eye-catching details and fine marks to create an amazing, unique effect. Try simple stars, C shapes, undulating lines, dashes, fish-scale patterns, straight lines, brickwork, patches of color, V shapes, and dots—whatever you can draw with a pencil, you can etch!

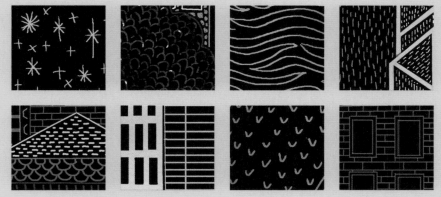

4. Use negative space

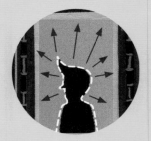

The black ink should be selectively removed—it can contribute to the final artwork if left alone. Leave areas of black behind, as shown with this silhouette framed in the window of an apartment block (page 12). Create an outline for the object you wish to draw, and then etch away from it, revealing the color background surrounding the shape.

The stylus
Keep one end for fine work and use the other point for applying more pressure.

5. Adding your interpretation

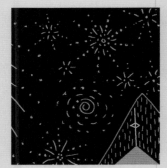

The background of each etching board is a place where you can choose what to etch and where. As you grow in confidence, you will find yourself freestyling in other areas too! Try etching splashes of color for fireworks, for example.

Make a different brick pattern on each building, or create reflections in the water. The more of the etch ink you remove from an area, the brighter a shape will be. Darker areas with finer details etched lightly retreat to create a stunning background.

Rio de Janeiro

Rio's mountainous skyline is dominated by the magnificent statue of Christ the Redeemer.

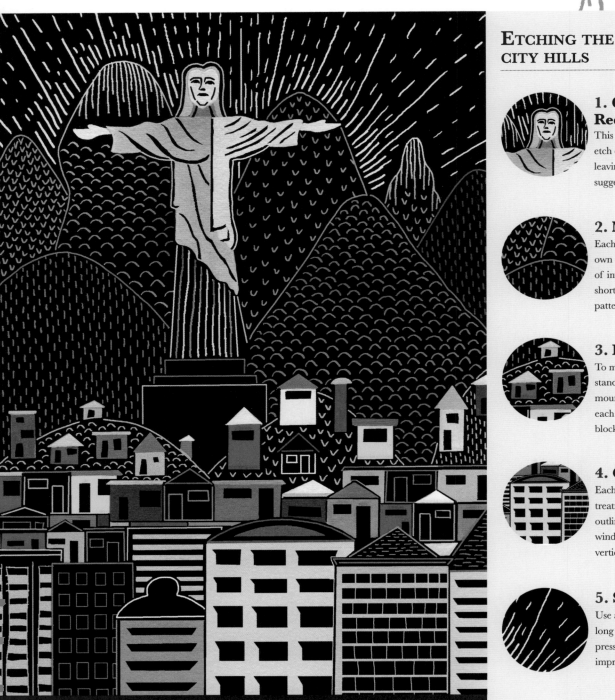

The finished view of Rio de Janeiro

ETCHING THE CITY HILLS

1. Christ the Redeemer
This statue has to stand out, so etch out most of the body, just leaving a few black lines to suggest folds of cloth.

2. Mountains
Each mountain should have its own character. Use a mixture of inverted U and V shapes, short dashes, and fish-scale patterns for each hill.

3. Favela
To make these smaller buildings stand out against the detailed mountains, fully scratch out each house to make a strong block of color.

4. City center
Each tower needs a different treatment. Once you have outlined them, mix large windows with small, and vertical lines with horizontal.

5. Sky
Use a mixture of short and long dashes, varying how much pressure you use, to give the impression of the rising sun.

4

When you have filled in this image, the contrast between natural
green textures and colorful man-made buildings will be simply stunning.

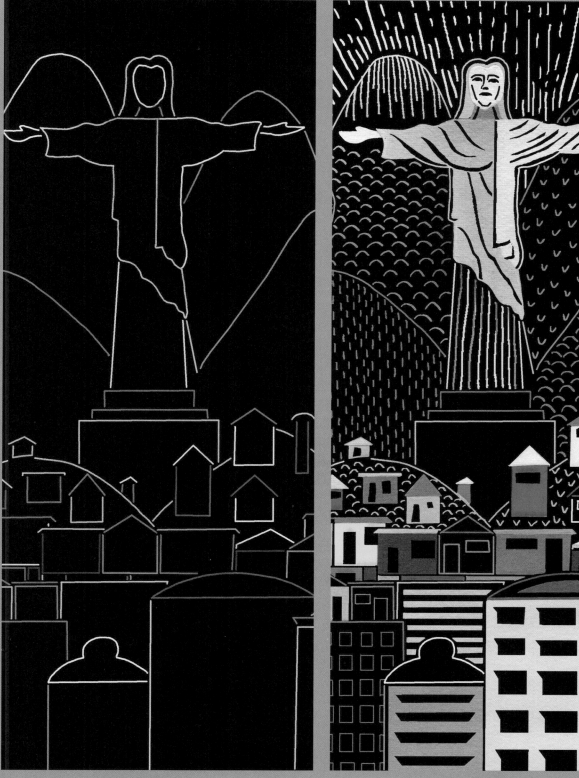

Before

After

② Barcelona

Antoni Gaudi's unique architecture, with its flowing lines and organic shapes, gives Barcelona its distinctive character.

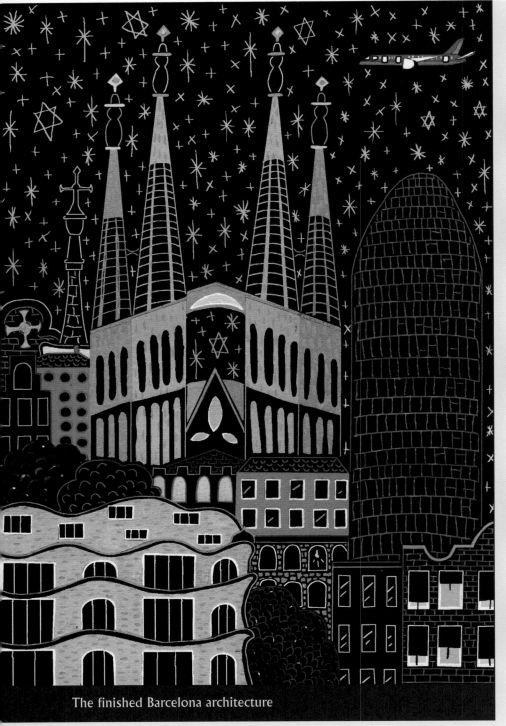

The finished Barcelona architecture

ETCHING A SPANISH CITYSCAPE

1. Sagrada Família
To make the cathedral stand out, etch out large sections of its main body, leaving black ovals in each section for the windows.

2. Cathedral spires
Outline these spires with a regular grid design, but use curved horizontal lines to give the impression of a rounded shape. Make them closer together the higher up the spire you go.

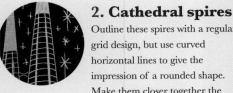

3. Torre Glòries
To create the facade of this Barcelona landmark, etch small rectangles to make windowpanes. Make them smaller at the top to give an impression of the building's curves.

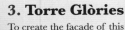

4. Sky
Fill the night sky with a mixture of twinkling stars—including five-pointed stars and stars made from overlapping triangles.

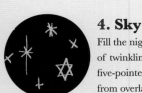

5. Trees
Use simple, upside-down U shapes placed at irregular intervals to create foliage. Change the thickness of the lines to add variety.

The cathedral dominates, but if you make a feature of the waving natural lines
on the building at the front of the picture, you can add balance to the scene.

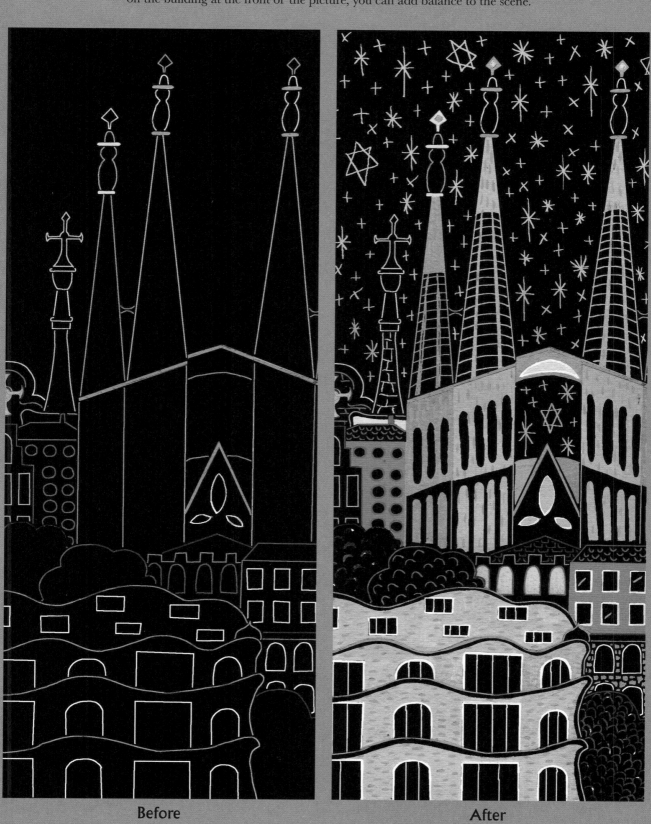

Before

After

3 Hong Kong

The towering skyscrapers symbolize this modern, bustling city, but there is still space for traditional culture in Hong Kong.

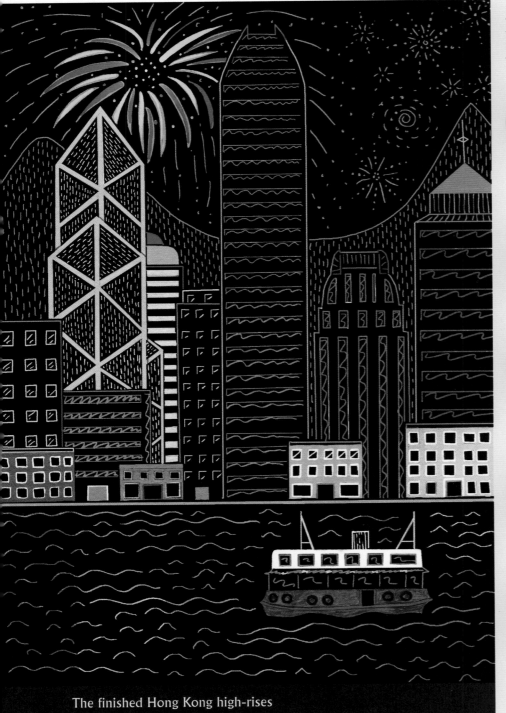

The finished Hong Kong high-rises

ETCHING THE SKYSCRAPERS

1. Bank of China Tower
Within each triangle shape, etch short lines to suggest the texture of small windows. Vary the angle and pressure of the lines in each triangle to add shape.

2. Harbor ferry
To make the boat pop out against the water, etch away the entire white top deck area, as well as the green hull.

3. Small tower
This smaller-scale building can be a simple contrast to the others. Create windowpane reflections by drawing two or three diagonal lines in each frame.

4. Hills
Create detail on the green hills behind the city with short, vertical lines. To suggest distance and shape, make the lines shorter at the top of each hill.

5. The night sky
Light up the sky with fireworks. Mix up wide, bold explosions of color with small, lively dashes at the end of each flare of light.

Use organic wavy lines to represent the choppy waters of the Hong Kong harbor, and etch straight lines and disciplined marks to show off the modern architecture of this 21st-century city.

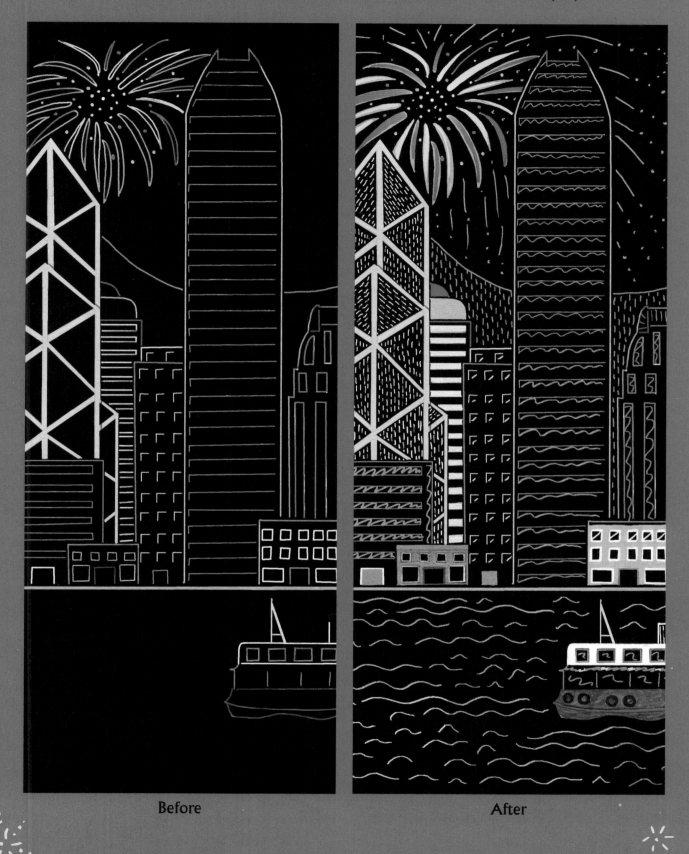

Before

After

4 New York

The city that never sleeps, with its unmistakable collection of remarkable skyscrapers and vast concrete canyons.

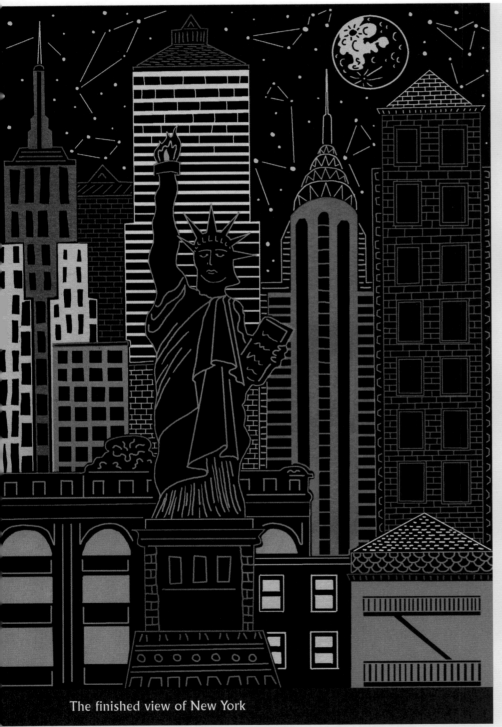

The finished view of New York

ETCHING ICONIC NEW YORK

1. Statue of Liberty
This is a great place to add contrasting softness and movement—draw lines to give the impression of draped cloth. Don't forget to add writing on her tablet.

2. Chrysler Building
Make sure you etch out the famous starburst features at the top of this art deco landmark. Carefully draw the zigzags on each layer of the pinnacle.

3. Grand Central
To create a grounded contrast to the tall skyscrapers, etch out large blocks of color to make solid window shapes.

4. Moon
Use a mixture of negative space (see page 3) and fine line work to create the craters and peaks.

5. Rooftop
Etch a horizontal fish-scale pattern to suggest tiles on the rectangular section, with short dashes on the upper rooftop to add interest and texture.

This busy cityscape has a great deal going on, so try to keep some areas simpler than others to offer some contrast—a solid block of color next to a brickwork tower works well.

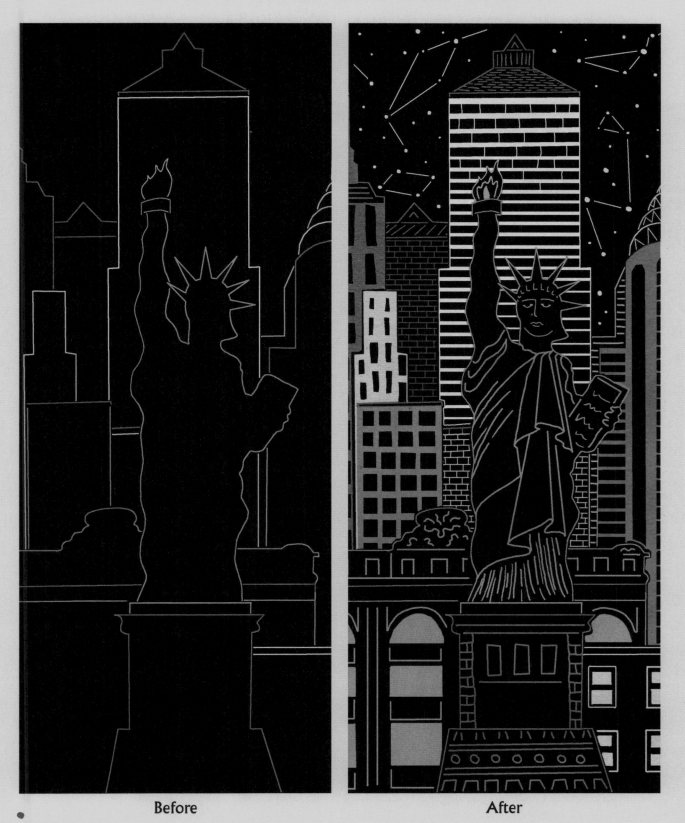

Before

After

5

Amsterdam

The tall, narrow townhouses lining the busy canal
are Amsterdam's most famous landmarks.

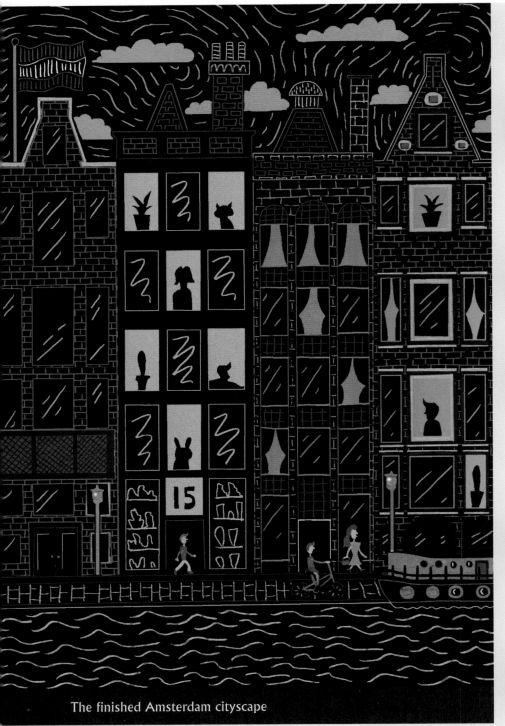

The finished Amsterdam cityscape

ETCHING THE CANALSIDE

1. Canal houses

Work the buildings with a brick
pattern, then etch one long
diagonal line across each
windowpane, with two smaller
lines on either side. Make sure
you vary the scale in each
window to avoid monotony.

2. Canal

Create eddies in the canal water
with curving, erratic lines to
give the water movement.

3. Sky

Etch a mixture of larger cloud
shapes, completely removing
the black inside the outline to
make them solid. Surround
them with short, curved lines
in a swirling pattern or add
your own interpretation of the
cloudy sky.

4. Silhouettes

These silhouetted figures
and objects are created using
the negative space technique
(see page 3). Outline the shape
you want, then work around it
to reveal the yellow areas.

5. Flag

Draw short, blunt, vertical lines
in rows to decorate the flag. Try
varying the density of the lines
to give the flag shape.

Create variation in each window by changing how you fill the space. Make closed or drawn drapes, or just a blank reflection—experiment with how you show a busy city block.

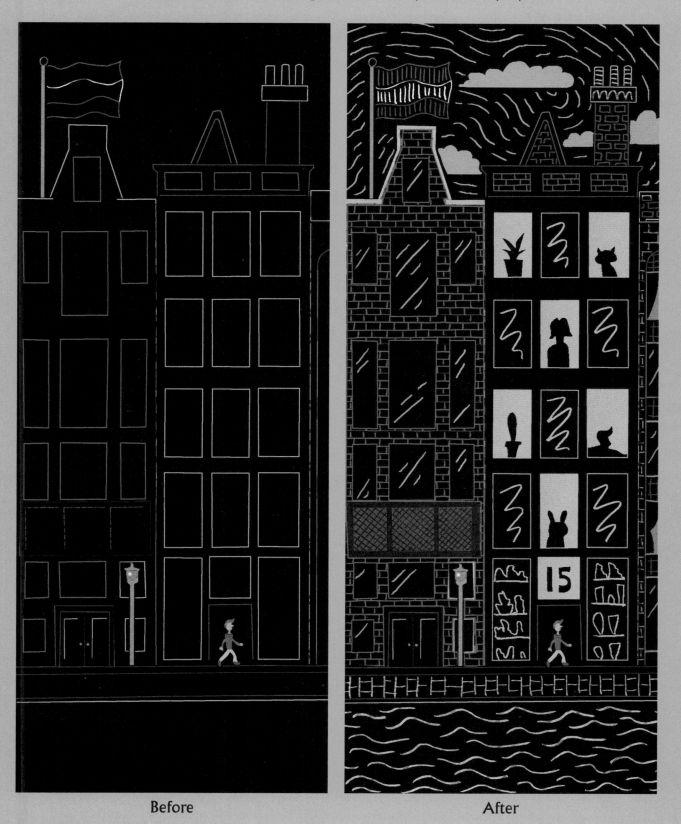

Before

After

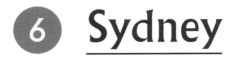

6 Sydney

Set on the banks of the world's largest natural harbor, Sydney is a city of golden beaches and startling architecture.

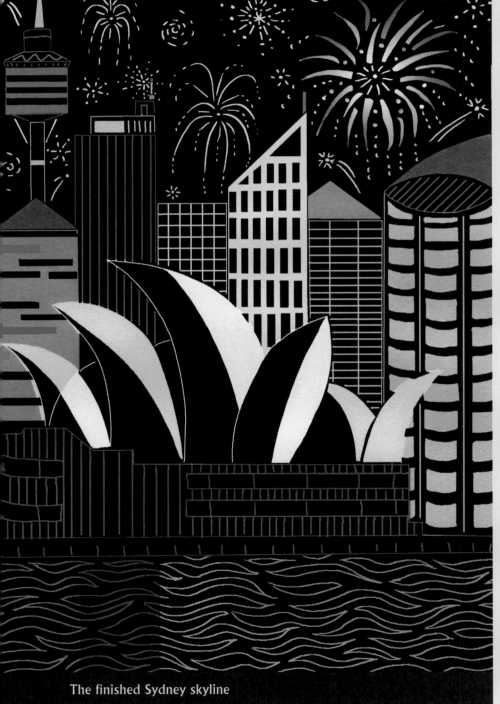

The finished Sydney skyline

ETCHING THE DISTINCTIVE CITY

1. Sydney Opera House roof

Create the unmistakable curves of the roof of the Opera House by etching out solid wedges of color. To ensure these shell shapes look three-dimensional, leave one curved side black to suggest shadow and light.

2. Sydney Opera House main building

As a contrast to the bold sails of the roof, treat the building with fine, vertical lines, leaving large areas of black behind.

3. Harbor

Create these sinuous, curved shapes with a hard line to show the choppy harbor waters.

4. Sydney Tower

Make sure the top of this tower doesn't get lost amid the fireworks by etching out strong, bold areas.

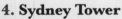

5. Fireworks

Use a mixture of soft and hard etched lines, dots, and dashes to give texture to the fireworks lighting up the Sydney sky.

Each skyscraper needs a different treatment to make them stand out.
Use a mixture of vertical and straight lines, and negative and positive space (see page 3).

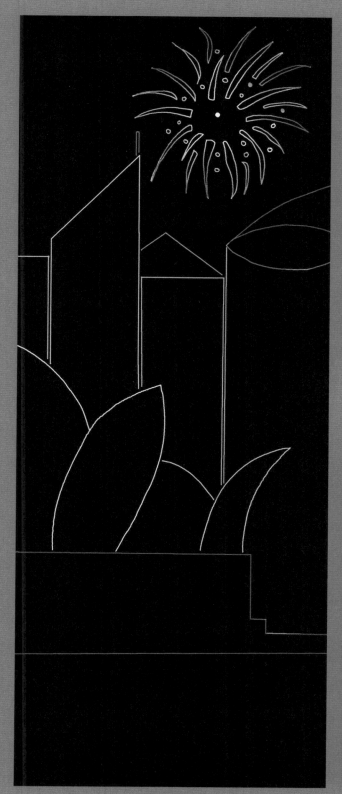

Before

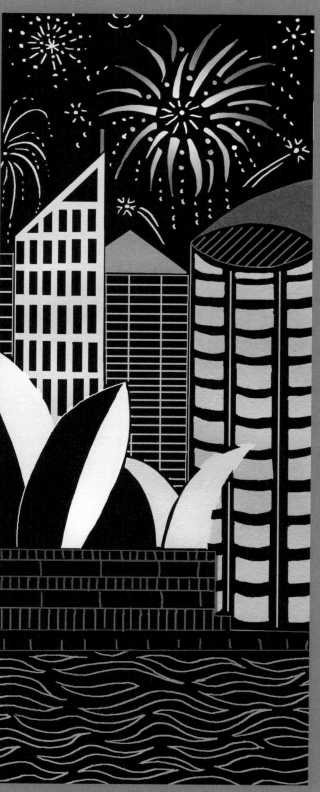

After

San Francisco

San Francisco is a mix of old and new, from 19th-century cable cars to its soaring skyscrapers.

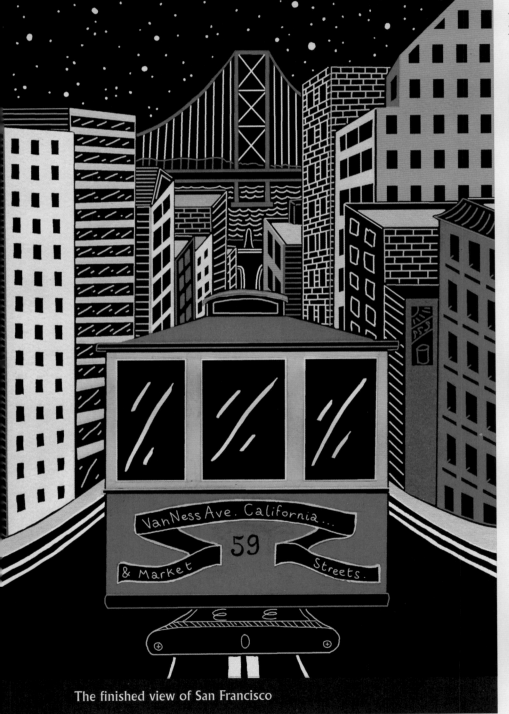

The finished view of San Francisco

ETCHING THE HILL VIEW

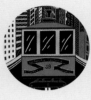

1. Cable car

There's no mistaking the boldly colored cable cars that travel through the city. Etch out most of the shape and use diagonal lines to create panes of glass.

2. Banner on the front of the cable car

A light touch is needed here. Choose a cable car name and etch it out carefully using fine, light strokes.

3. Golden Gate Bridge

To accentuate the symmetry of this suspension bridge, use regular straight lines to make the strong cables and girders.

4. Skyscraper

Use negative space (see page 3) for the windows and a mixture of wide and narrow lines to etch out this skyscraper. To mimic reflections in the glass, add short diagonal strokes.

5. Advertising hoarding

Leave an area of negative space (see page 3) on this building and etch out a fine copy of an old-fashioned advertisement.

These skyscrapers crowd together, so keep them
distinct by giving each one a different treatment.

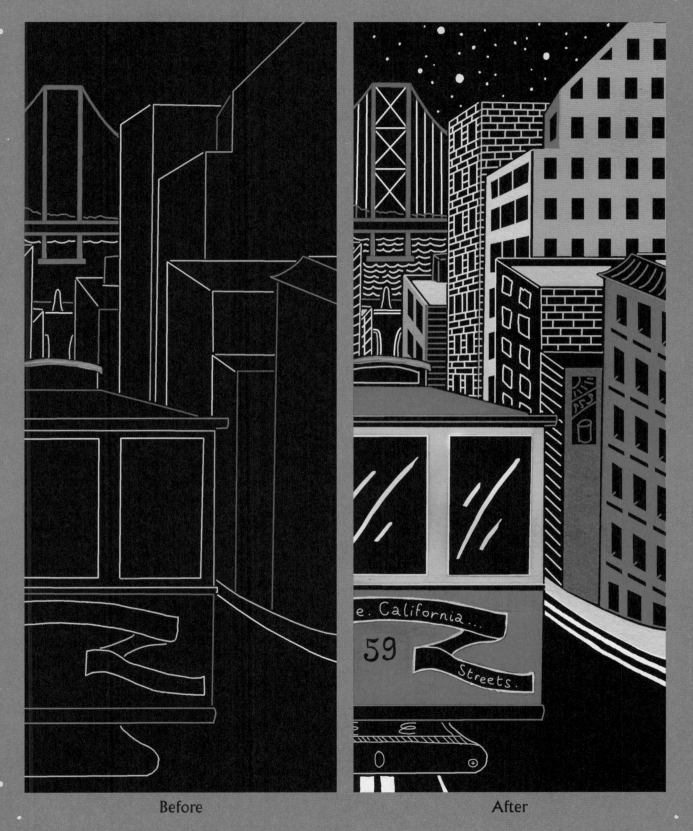

Before

After

17

Rome

The ancient past is never far away in Rome, with classical ruins that rub shoulders with Renaissance wonders of architecture.

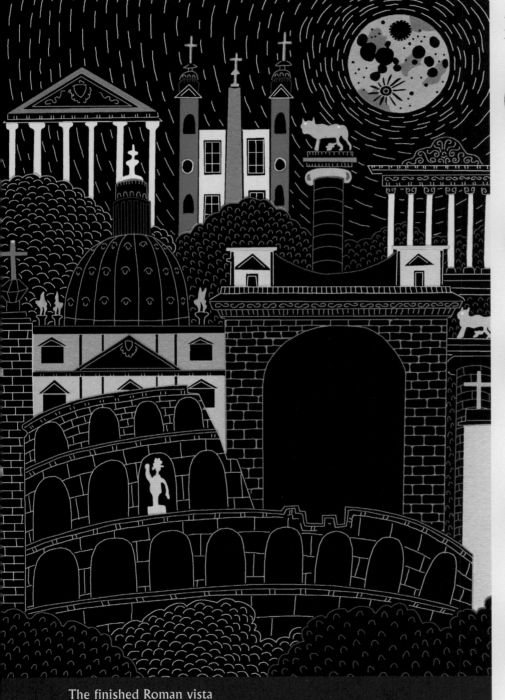

The finished Roman vista

ETCHING THE HISTORIC CITY

1. Colosseum
Etch out the lines of stonework that make up this Roman icon, leaving the archways dark. Keep the lines of the stonework irregular, and smaller at the top than the bottom.

2. St. Peter's Basilica
Ensure the Vatican church isn't lost in this busy scene by etching out its base completely, leaving windows and entablatures dark.

3. Arch of Constantine
While the base is kept simple, the frieze at the top of the arch can be rendered in different types of fine detail. Mix S shapes with dashes to create classical motifs.

4. Trajan's Column
Etch out the statue of Romulus and Remus and the wolf entirely, so the golden symbol of Rome stands out.

5. Forum
Roman architecture is all about order, so etch the Forum's columns with disciplined, straight lines.

As a contrast to the heavy architecture, keep the foliage light.
Mix small U-shaped marks of varying sizes to suggest different trees.

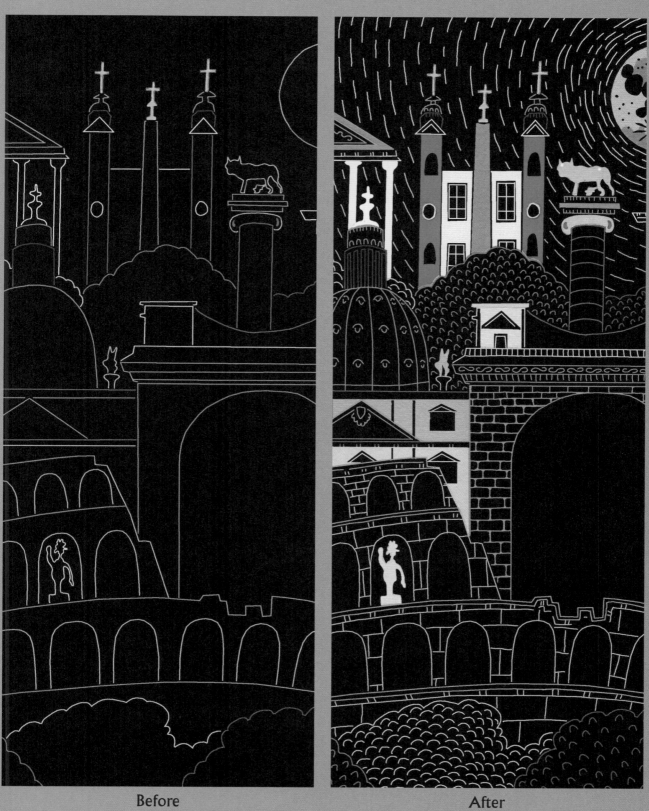

Before

After

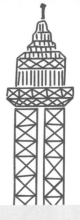

9 Paris

Wide boulevards and elegant architecture epitomize Paris—you are never far from a tree-lined square.

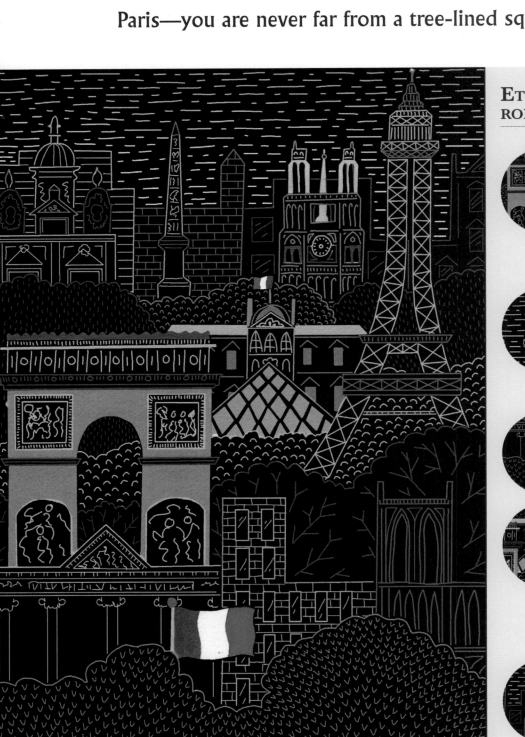

The finished Parisian architecture

ETCHING THE CITY OF ROMANCE

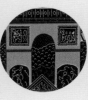

1. Arc de Triomphe
Use finely etched lines with light, delicate strokes for the classical tableaux. Etch out the main body of the arch to give it weight.

2. Eiffel Tower
To create the strict geometrical shapes of this steel edifice, make strong, symmetrical lines to show the steel girders.

3. Tricolore
This flag needs to stand out, so etch out each section completely.

4. Louvre
Use the negative space technique (see page 3) to etch out the diamond-shaped window panels of the Louvre pyramid. Make them smaller at the top to make it look more three-dimensional.

5. Notre-Dame
Make sure this Gothic masterpiece doesn't fade into the background by adding plenty of detail. Mix heavy lines with fine details to re-create the elaborate facade.

Paris is famous for its chestnut trees. Make a dramatic feature of the various areas of foliage
by filling it with U and V shapes of varying sizes, dashes, or etch lines for branches.

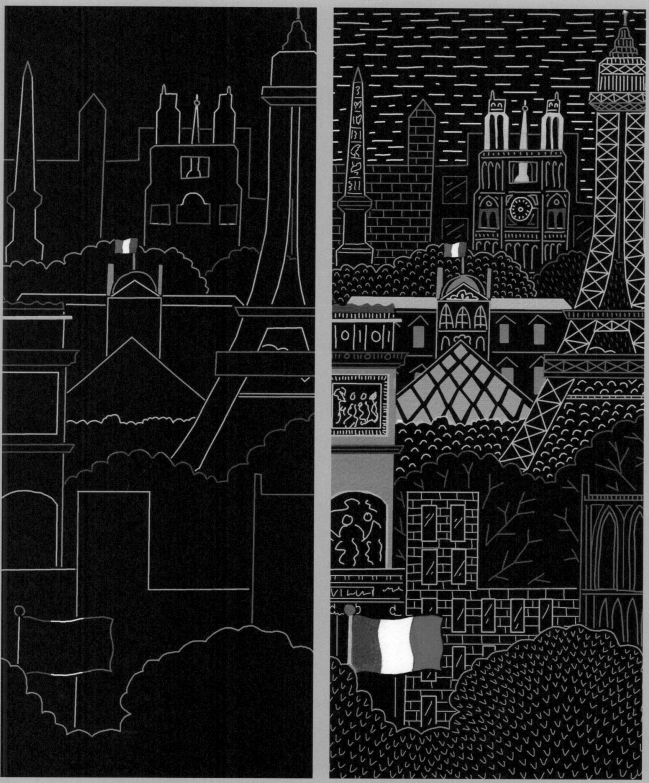

Before

After

10 London

A city filled with design icons from every era—from Westminster to the postmodern towers of Canary Wharf.

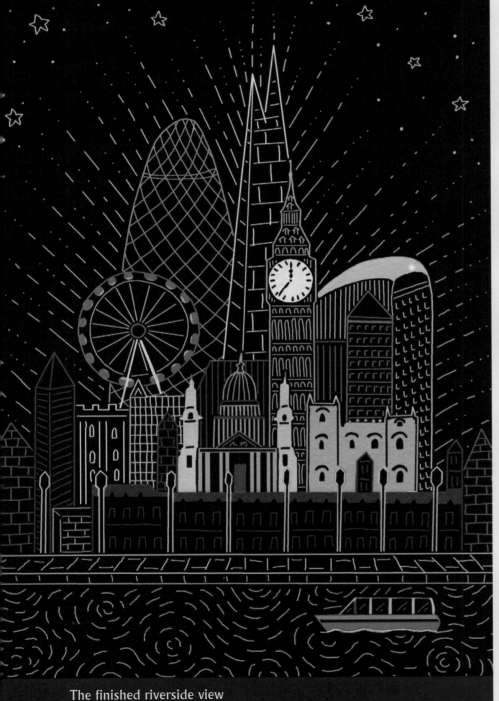

The finished riverside view

ETCHING THE CITY

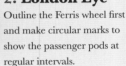

1. Big Ben
Use a mixture of detailed fine lines for this intricate Gothic bell tower, and use the negative space technique (see page 3) for the clock face.

2. London Eye
Outline the Ferris wheel first and make circular marks to show the passenger pods at regular intervals.

3. Gherkin
To give the impression of lightness of design, use fine strokes to outline the curved diagonal pattern on this famous landmark.

4. St. Paul's Cathedral
Combine thick, straight lines with lighter details on the dome to give this cathedral its distinctive classical facade. Etch out the wing towers in their entirety to give them weight.

5. Tower of London
To give the impression of a strong fortress, etch out most of the castle walls, leaving only small window shapes behind.

22

Add your own interpretation to the waters of the Thames. Choose swirling circles or go for something more sedate with calm, curved lines.

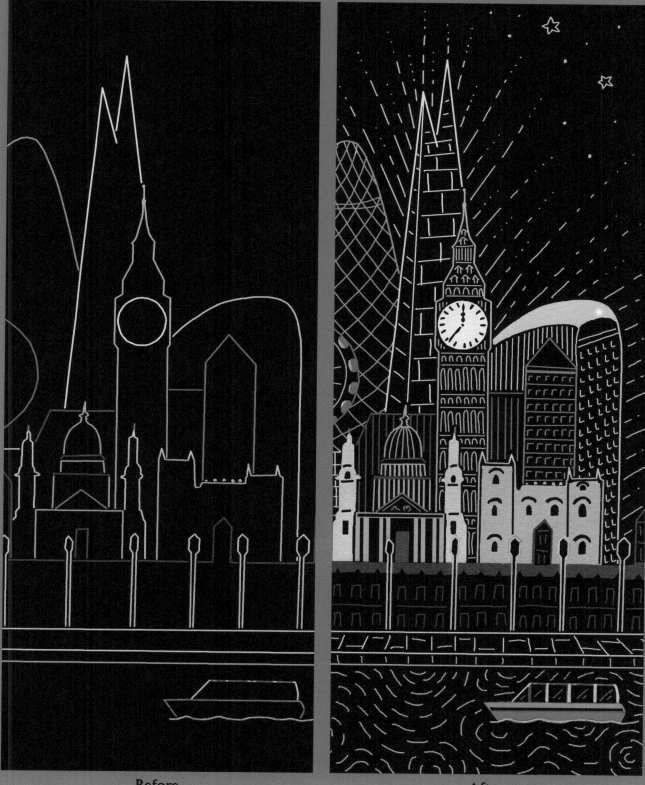

Before

After

The Artful Etching Cities

The boards in the following section can be removed from the book for easy use. Gently pull the boards out of the book to use the instructions at the same time. Page numbers below give a reminder of where to find the instructions.

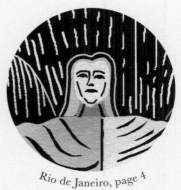

Rio de Janeiro, page 4

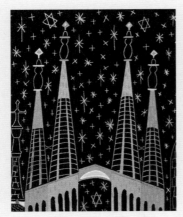

Barcelona, page 6

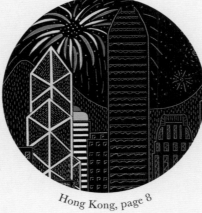

Hong Kong, page 8

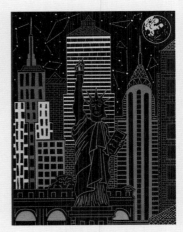

New York, page 10

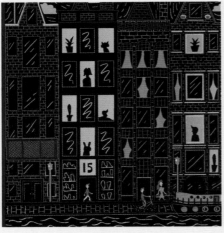

Amsterdam, page 12

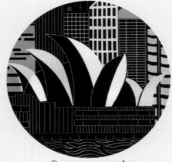

Sydney, page 14

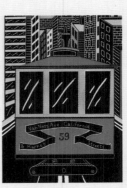

San Francisco, page 16

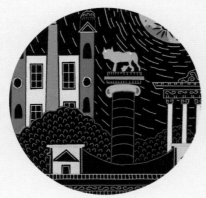

Rome, page 18

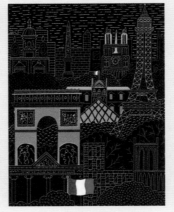

Paris, page 20

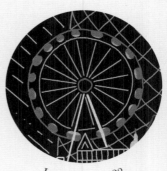

London, page 22

24

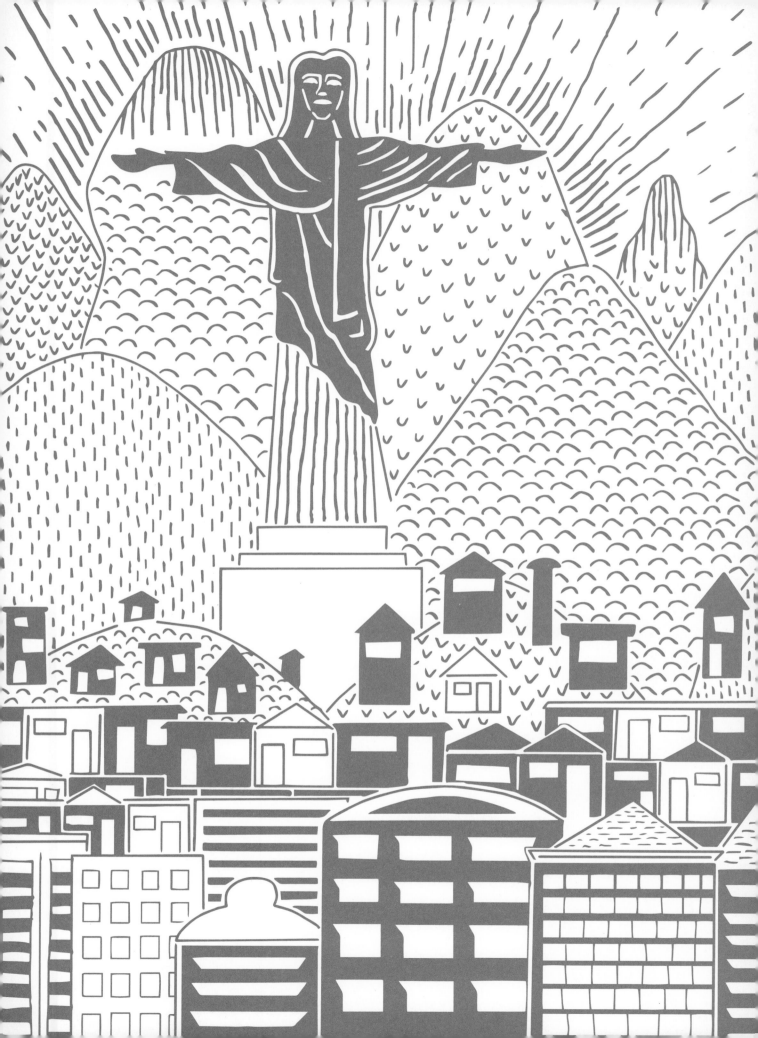

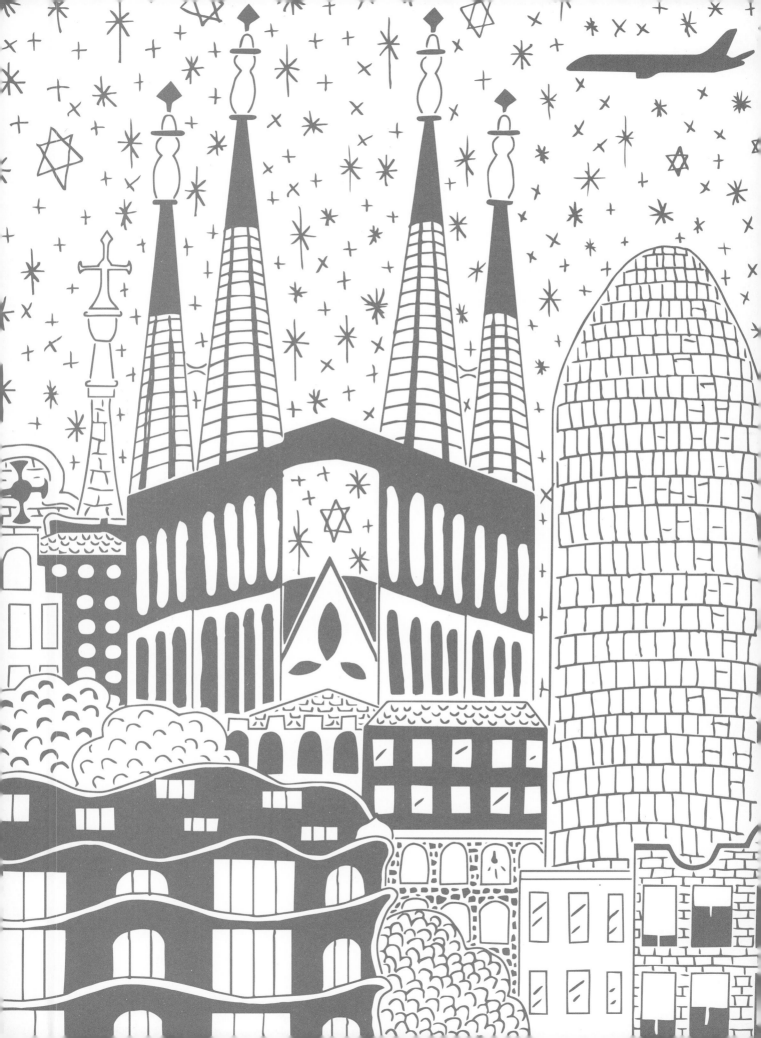

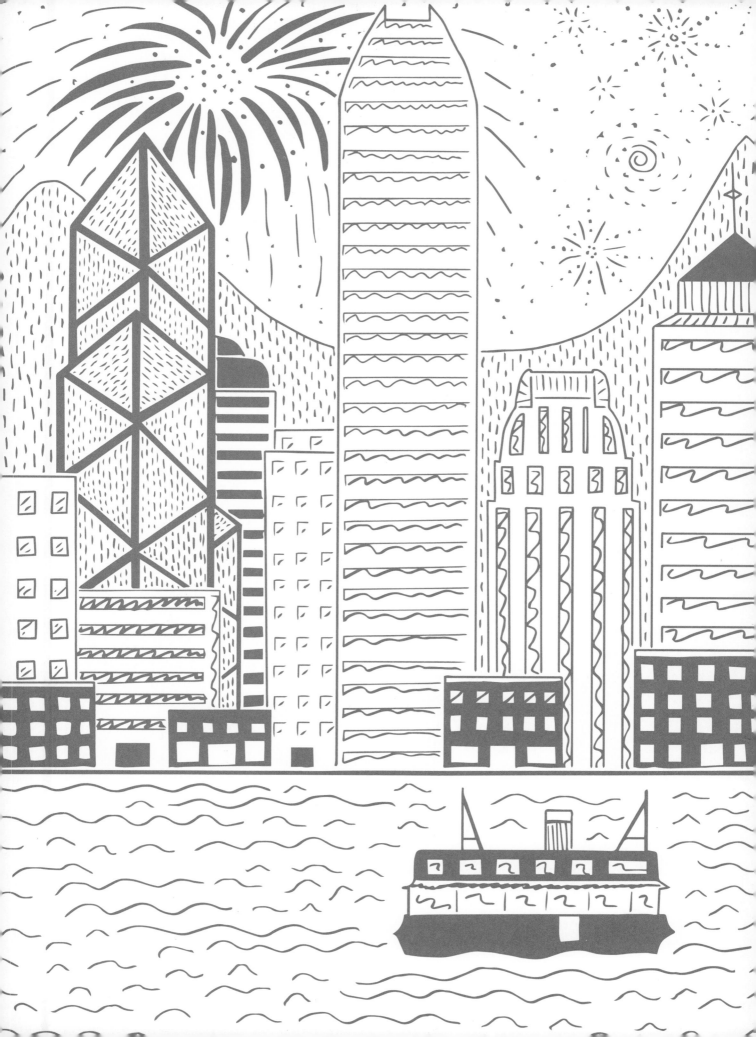

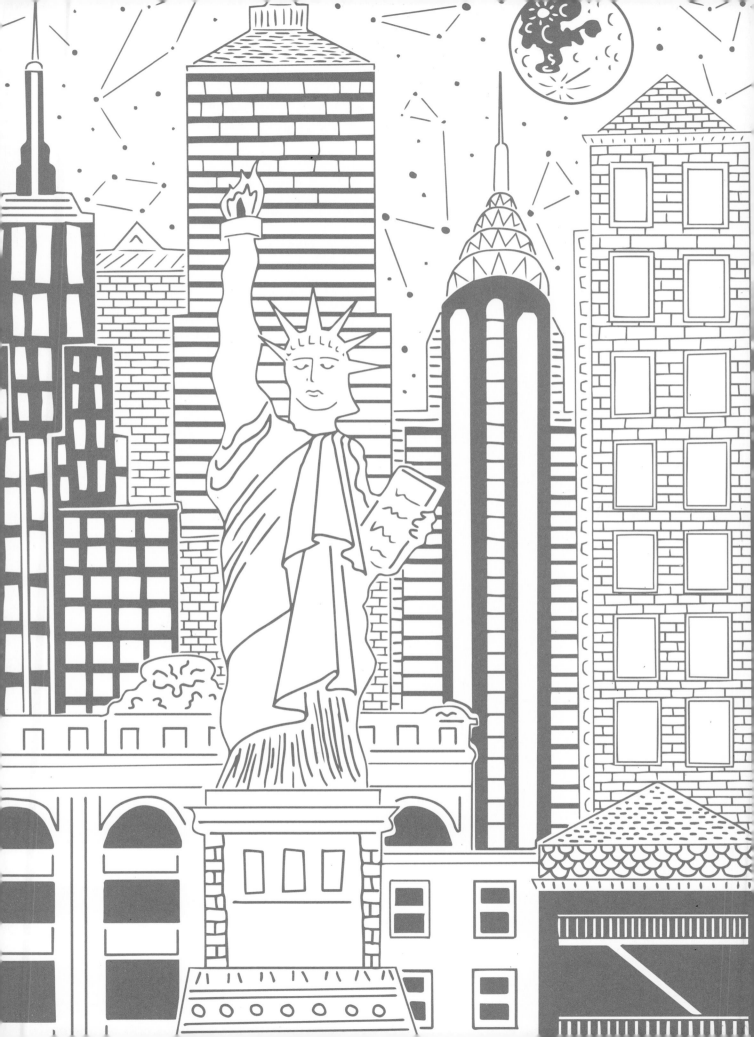

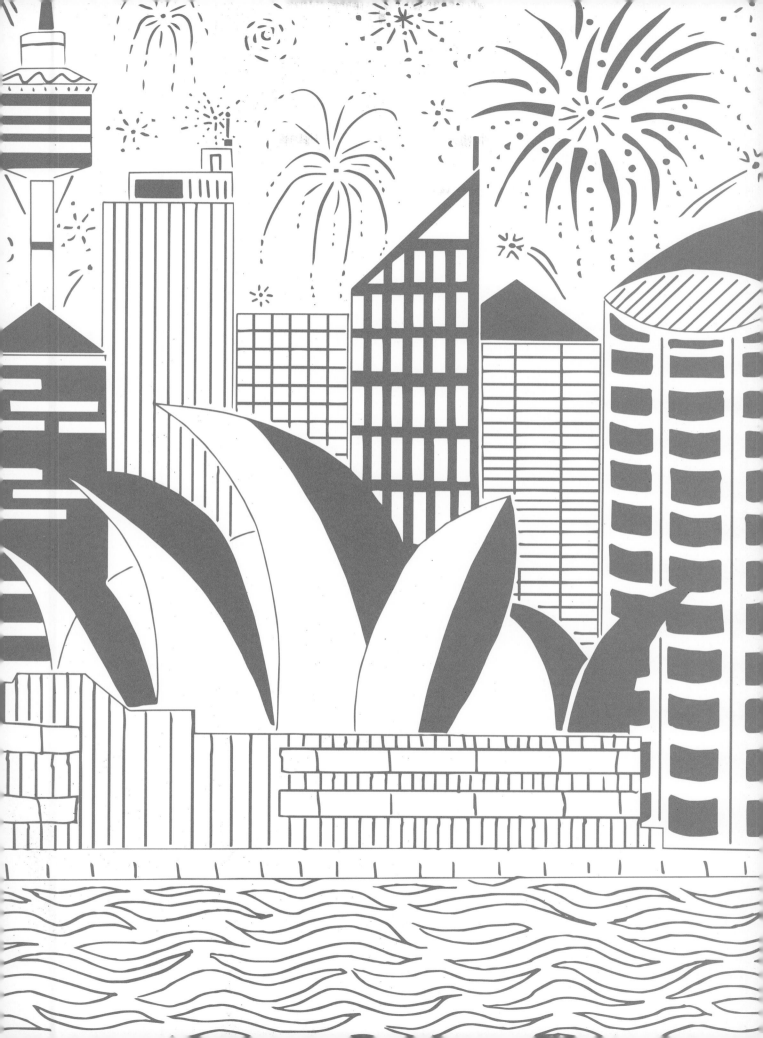